STOCK CARS

MotoR Mania

by Matt Doeden

William Burt, stock car racing consultant and
author of several books on motor sports

Lerner Publications Company • Minneapolis

For Mom

Cover Photo: Ryan Newman sits at the head of the pack at the Phoenix International Raceway in Arizona.

Lerner Publications Company
A division of Lerner Publishing Group
241 First Avenue North
Minneapolis, MN 55401 U.S.A.

Website address: www.lernerbooks.com

Library of Congress Cataloging-in-Publication Data

Doeden, Matt.
    Stock cars / by Matt Doeden.
        p.   cm. — (Motor Mania)
    Includes bibliographical references and index.
    ISBN-13: 978–0–8225–3530–0 (lib. bdg. : alk. paper)
    ISBN-10: 0–8225–3530–0 (lib. bdg. : alk. paper)
    1. Stock cars (Automobiles)—Juvenile literature.
    2. Stock car racing—Juvenile literature. I. Title.
    II. Series: Motor Mania (Minneapolis, Minn.)
    TL236.28.D64 2007
    629.228—dc22   2005019321

Manufactured in the United States of America
1 2 3 4 5 6 – DP – 12 11 10 09 08 07

Contents

Introduction

Stock cars are powerful racing machines. Common stock car models include the Chevrolet Monte Carlo, the Dodge Charger, and the Ford Fusion. Early stock cars came from the same production, or stock, as the cars people bought and drove every day. Modern stock car racing teams custom build (build just for racing) almost all the body and engine parts for a stock car. They work to make the cars faster and safer than road cars. Teams even add special tires called slicks that are designed to get the best grip on a track's surface.

NASCAR® (National Association of Stock Car Automobile Racing) organizes most of the stock car races in the United States. NASCAR sponsors many racing events, from small dirt-track racing series to the highest level of racing, the Nextel Cup.

NASCAR racing is one of the fastest-growing and most exciting sports in the United States. Millions of fans show up to watch the races at tracks across the country. Millions more watch the competition on television. Stock cars are fast, loud, and colorful. Stock car races are a thrill to watch.

Drivers fight for the lead position during an early lap of a race at Infineon Raceway in Sonoma, California.

Chapter One

STOCK CAR HISTORY

A 1920s bootlegger uses a smoke machine to try to escape from motorcycle cops.

Racing became popular in the United States in the early 1900s. In 1919, the United States passed a law outlawing the drinking of alcohol. Under Prohibition (1920–1933), people who illegally made or sold alcohol were called bootleggers. They needed fast cars to outrun law enforcement officials. Bootleggers often made changes to their cars to make them faster. They called their cars "runners."

Some of these bootleggers argued about whose runner was the fastest. They held races to find out. Soon the races became organized. People gathered to watch the bootleggers and their fast runners. Before long, people built oval tracks just for racing. The earliest form of stock car racing had begun.

Stock car racing grew more popular in the 1930s and early 1940s. Soon racetracks could be found all over the United States, especially in the South. Racetracks charged fans to watch the races and offered cash prizes to the race winners. Some drivers traveled from track to track, trying to earn enough prize money to make a living.

By the late 1940s, the sport had a big problem. Each track owner set the rules for races at that track. The rules were different at every track. Drivers and fans were often confused.

NASCAR Is Born

In 1947, a driver and racing promoter named Bill France decided to do something about the different rules.

Spectators watch stock cars race through the sands of Daytona Beach, Florida, in 1936. Daytona Beach has been a hotspot for racing since the early 1900s.

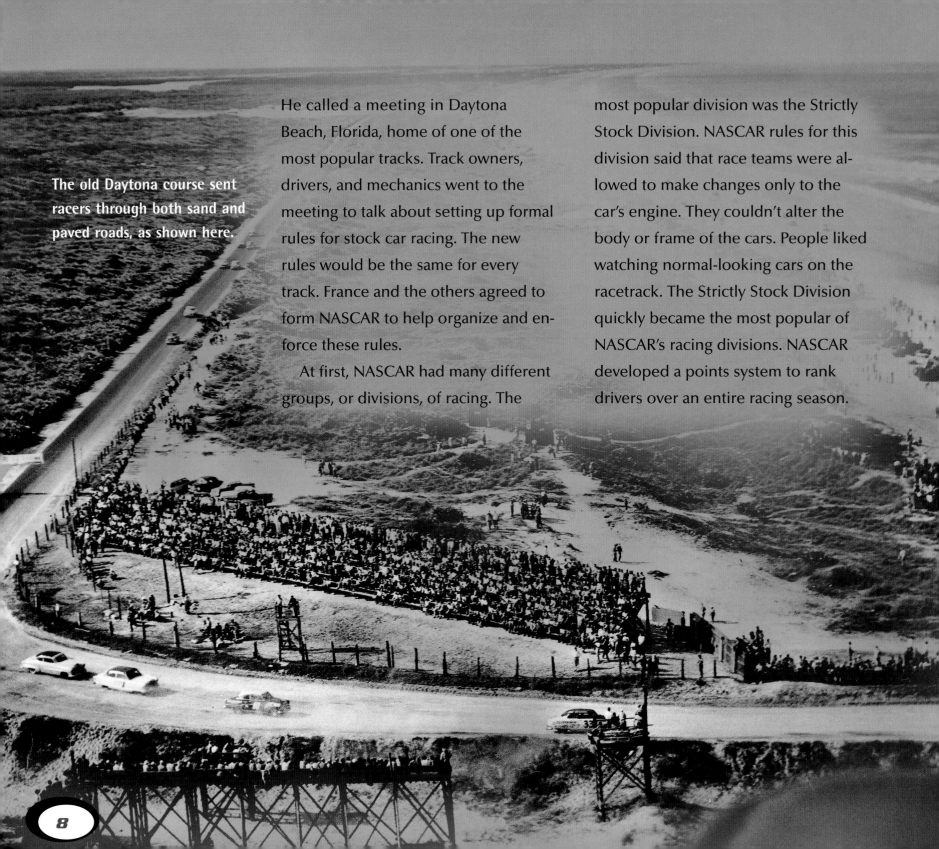

The old Daytona course sent racers through both sand and paved roads, as shown here.

He called a meeting in Daytona Beach, Florida, home of one of the most popular tracks. Track owners, drivers, and mechanics went to the meeting to talk about setting up formal rules for stock car racing. The new rules would be the same for every track. France and the others agreed to form NASCAR to help organize and enforce these rules.

At first, NASCAR had many different groups, or divisions, of racing. The most popular division was the Strictly Stock Division. NASCAR rules for this division said that race teams were allowed to make changes only to the car's engine. They couldn't alter the body or frame of the cars. People liked watching normal-looking cars on the racetrack. The Strictly Stock Division quickly became the most popular of NASCAR's racing divisions. NASCAR developed a points system to rank drivers over an entire racing season.

Drivers earn points based on where they finish in each race.

At first, almost all NASCAR racing was on small dirt tracks. But in 1950, a paved oval track opened in Darlington, South Carolina. Darlington Raceway changed stock car racing forever. Within a few years, small, paved ovals began appearing all around the South. NASCAR races became big events. Tens of thousands of fans filled the stands for races. Within just a few years, the popularity of stock car racing had exploded.

Soon car companies such as Ford, Chevrolet, and Dodge realized that people were paying attention to which cars won the most races. The companies all wanted their cars to be the best. Having a winning car was good for business. The car companies began building cars just for racing. They gave them bigger engines and stronger, sleeker frames. They built them for superior speed, handling, and safety. Some car companies had a

saying, "Win on Sunday, sell on Monday." They believed success on the track led to sales of their cars.

In 1955, Chevrolet introduced a new kind of engine called a small block V8. The V8 gave drivers speed and acceleration that they'd never had before. Soon other car companies added similar engines. The new, faster cars thrilled the fans. In 1956, 60,000 people gathered at Darlington, South Carolina, to watch the Southern 500. With the power of

Bill France *(left)* ran NASCAR for almost 25 years. Nicknamed Big Bill, he earned a reputation for doing things his way. France admitted that he could be stubborn but said that he always looked out for the good of the sport. When France stepped down in 1971, his son, Bill France Jr., took over for him.

the V8 under the hood, drivers such as Buck Baker and Lee Petty dominated the sport during the late 1950s.

A Changing Sport

NASCAR realized that teams needed to be able to make more changes to the cars. As the sport became more popular, new and bigger racetracks began springing up. On small tracks, cars had to slow down for turns. But cars on large tracks could tear around the turns at high speeds. This made for exciting racing, but it also put drivers in greater danger. At these speeds, a car body that was "strictly stock" was no longer safe. Race teams needed to add special tires and more safety features such as roll cages.

As the 1960s began, a new kind of paved track called a superspeedway changed the sport. Superspeedways were huge tracks, often more than two miles (3.2 km) around. The most famous of these was Daytona International Speedway in Daytona, Florida.

Cars roar around the track during the first Daytona 500 race in February 1959. The leading car, Number 42, belongs to Lee Petty. Petty, the father of NASCAR wins leader Richard Petty, won the race.

How an Internal Combustion Engine Works

All NASCAR race cars have internal combustion V8 engines. A V8 is an engine that includes eight cylinders arranged in the shape of a *V*. Like most car engines, they run on gasoline and use a four stroke cycle. The four stroke cycle burns a mixture of air and gas to power the car. These cycles take place thousands of times inside a car engine.

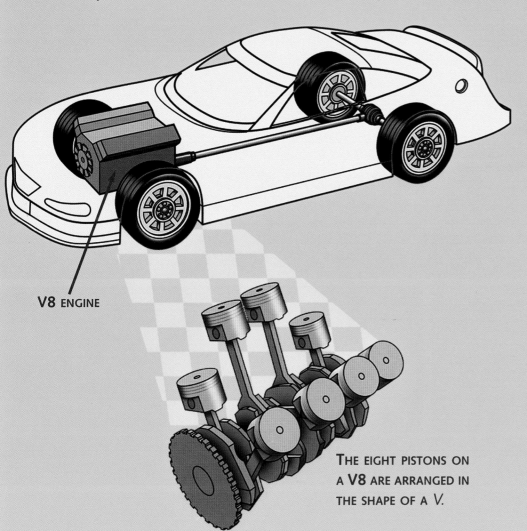

V8 ENGINE

THE EIGHT PISTONS ON A V8 ARE ARRANGED IN THE SHAPE OF A *V*.

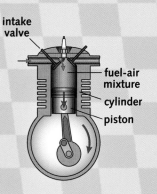

1. INTAKE STROKE
The piston moves down the cylinder and draws the fuel-air mixture into the cylinder through the intake valve.

intake valve
fuel-air mixture
cylinder
piston

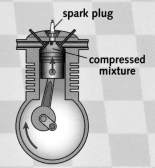

2. COMPRESSION STROKE
The piston moves up and compresses the fuel-air mixture. The spark plug ignites the mixture, creating combustion (burning).

spark plug
compressed mixture

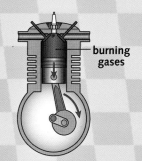

3. POWER STROKE
The burning gases created by combustion push the piston downward. This gives the engine its power.

burning gases

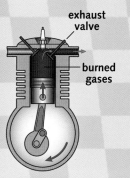

4. EXHAUST STROKE
The piston moves up again and pushes out the burned-out exhaust gases through the exhaust valve.

exhaust valve
burned gases

The Daytona track is so large that an entire lake lies in the center.

Superspeedway racing was a completely new kind of racing. Cars could pass one another more easily. They could race two and three wide without crashing. The turns were so wide and long that drivers hardly ever had to use their brakes. Drivers and teams had to find new ways of setting up their cars to win.

Stock car racing began to rival the popular sport of IndyCar racing, which had been made famous by the Indianapolis 500. During the 1960s, many of NASCAR's top drivers became celebrities. Richard Petty, David Pearson, and others soon became very well known. Fans could watch the biggest races, including the Daytona 500, on television. NASCAR had grown from a small, regional sport into a major business with a huge fan base across the United States.

Throughout the 1960s, racing

teams and car companies made improvements to cars. They tried new engines, new body styles, and new tires. By around 1970, the look and setup of different stock car models was about the same. Since then, stock cars have continued to evolve. The biggest changes have been to the cars' size and shape. Over the years, the cars have gotten smaller and more aerodynamic. They move through the air very easily.

Building Safer Cars

In the 1970s, Richard Petty and Cale Yarborough dominated competition.

Richard Petty

Richard Petty *(right)* is by far the most successful driver in NASCAR history. The North Carolina native won 200 races and seven points championships over his 27-year career. His father Lee, son Kyle, and grandson Adam all enjoyed successful racing careers.

Racers scream around the track during the first lap of the 1962 Daytona 500.

Richard Petty's car rolls during a massive wreck at Darlington Raceway in 1970.

During the 1980s, Dale Earnhardt and Darrell Waltrip were the top drivers. Earnhardt's hard-charging style earned him the nickname The Intimidator. He was never afraid to bump another car to move it out of his way. Earnhardt won several championships and was tremendously popular. Meanwhile, the cars kept changing shape to match the popular styles of the times, and the competition remained fierce.

The most important changes to stock cars during this time were for safety. Stock cars had become so powerful that they could reach dangerous speeds on large tracks such as Daytona and the Talladega Superspeedway in Alabama. Crashes at these tracks were very risky to drivers. They were also a danger to fans, because car parts could fly into the stands and injure people.

To slow down the cars at these tracks, NASCAR forced teams to add metal restrictor plates to the engines. The restrictor plates cut down the amount of air that can flow into the en- gines. With less air, the engines cannot burn fuel as quickly, and the cars slow down. For years, NASCAR teams had been trying only to go faster and faster. The restrictor plate was the first big change to slow down cars.

In the early 1990s, NASCAR officials tackled another problem. When a driver loses control at high speed, the car often spins around and slides back- ward. Cars that were sliding backward were unstable. They could easily lift off the ground, putting drivers and fans in

A NASCAR restrictor plate. The plates slow down cars by cutting down the amount of air the engine can receive.

Dale Earnhardt pulls ahead of challengers during his first NASCAR championship season in 1980.

Jeff Gordon

danger. NASCAR came up with a simple safety solution. They added roof flaps to the cars. The roof flaps pop up when a car spins around. The flaps help to slow the car and prevent it from flying off the track.

The 1990s saw the rise of another superstar driver—Jeff Gordon. Young, baby-faced, and very talented, Gordon won his first championship in 1995. He has won three more since then and remains one of NASCAR's top drivers and biggest stars.

In 2000, two popular NASCAR driv-ers were killed when their throttles be-came stuck. The throttle controls how much fuel goes into the engine. Adam Petty (grandson of the legendary Richard Petty) and Kenny Irwin were both killed in crashes because they couldn't slow down their cars. After their deaths, NASCAR decided to force teams to add kill switches to the steer-ing wheels of their cars. The kill switch is a button that instantly turns off the engine. A driver who feels the throttle sticking can hit the button to save the car and driver.

Roof flaps pop out when a car begins to slide sideways or backwards. The flaps cut down the air flowing over the car to keep it from lifting off the ground.

A Terrible Loss

In 2001, Dale Earnhardt was racing in the Daytona 500. At the age of 49, he was nearing the end of a long and successful career. Over the years, The Intimidator had won seven championships with his Number 3 car. His young son Dale Earnhardt Jr. looked like he was going to carry on the family's winning tradition.

On the final lap of the 2001 Daytona 500, Earnhardt was battling with Sterlin Marlin for third place. In the final turn, they made contact. Earnhardt's car spun. Ken Schrader ran into him from behind. Both cars smashed into the outside wall of the track. Schrader quickly got out of his car. Earnhardt did not. The crash didn't look that bad to many of the fans. They were busy cheering as Michael Waltrip held off Dale Earnhardt Jr. for the win. But the crowd soon grew silent as emergency crews rushed to the crashed cars. Later, the world learned that Earnhardt had died instantly of head injuries. NASCAR had lost its top driver.

Dale Earnhardt *(inset)* and his black Number 3 car *(bottom)* dominated NASCAR for much of the 1980s and 1990s. Earnhardt's popularity rivaled even Richard Petty's.

NASCAR quickly decided that drivers needed better protection from head injuries. They created a rule that all drivers must wear a Head and Neck Support (HANS) device. This is a system that holds a driver's head in place during a crash. The HANS and other new safety features have made stock car racing safer than ever.

The Chase

The year 2004 saw big changes for NASCAR. For years, NASCAR's top stock car division was the Winston Cup. But in 2004, a communications company called Nextel bought the rights to name the series. The Winston Cup became the Nextel Cup.

That wasn't the only change of 2004, though. NASCAR officials also decided it was time to change the way the sport decides its champion. The Nextel Cup is a series. Its teams compete in 36 races. Winning races is important. But having many good finishes is also important. Nextel Cup drivers earn points for every race they take part in. A win is worth 180 points. A 43rd-place finish is worth only 34 points. Drivers also earn five bonus points for leading a lap. They earn five more points if they lead the most laps of the race. To win a championship, a driver needs to perform well in as many races as possible.

Under the old Winston Cup rules, NASCAR added up each driver's total points over the season. But this system had a big problem. Sometimes a driver would build up such a big points lead that nobody had a chance to catch up to him. Having a driver clinch the championship with several weeks left was bad for the sport. NASCAR wanted to make the last races of the season more meaningful and exciting. They wanted a playoff system like those in other sports.

NASCAR's idea was to split up the racing season. The first 26 races of the year are the sport's regular season.

The HANS system attaches to the driver's helmet. It keeps the driver's head from snapping around violently during a crash.

At the end of 26 races, the top 10 drivers (and anyone else within 400 points of the leader) enter a 10-race "Chase for the Cup."

In 2004, five drivers entered the final race with a chance to win the championship. Kurt Busch won by only eight points over Jimmie Johnson. It was the closest Cup finish in history. Under the old rules, Busch would have finished fourth and Jeff Gordon would have won by 67 points over Johnson.

The Chase for the Cup system has given NASCAR the boost it was looking for. The new system adds extra excitement to the last 10 races. Every driver who competes in the Chase knows that one mistake—a bad race, a wreck, or an engine failure—can ruin their championship hopes in a hurry. Meanwhile, a little good luck and some great races give every Chase driver a chance to win it all. The Chase for the Cup promises to keep NASCAR fans on the edge of their seats for a long, long time.

Stock cars pile up during a Nextel Cup race at Infineon Raceway.

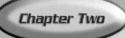

Chapter Two

STOCK CAR CULTURE

Stock car racing is a big business. The prize money for winning some races is more than $1 million. Kurt Busch and his team earned a bonus of more than $5 million for winning the 2004 Nextel Cup. Racing teams earn even more money through sponsorships. Top stock cars are like high-powered billboards. They're painted to advertise tools, cereals, phone companies, candy, and more. Teams earn sponsorship money by allowing companies to advertise their products on their cars and uniforms.

The highest level of stock car racing is NASCAR's Nextel Cup. Nextel Cup drivers compete over a 10-month season that begins in February with the Daytona 500. Drivers and teams travel all around the United States. Most

races are held in the South. But the series also travels to tracks in California, Illinois, Nevada, Kansas, and more.

The Nextel Cup isn't NASCAR's only racing series. The Busch Series is a lower level of stock car racing. Busch Series races often take place the day before a Nextel Cup race. NASCAR also sponsors many small local and regional stock car racing series. NASCAR even has a series for trucks called the Craftsman Truck Series.

The Race

A driver's first job at the track is to qualify for the race. For most races, qualifying is held on a Friday afternoon. The race is held that Sunday.

Cars stream onto a packed pit road at Phoenix International Raceway in Arizona.

To qualify, each driver runs two laps alone on the track. Officials time each lap. Whichever driver has the fastest time earns the pole, the first starting spot in the race. The remaining drivers line up based on their qualifying times. A few spots at the back of the field are reserved for the top drivers. These spots ensure that the fans get to see all of their favorites, even if a driver has a bad qualifying run.

After qualifying, the race field of 43 drivers is set. On Saturday the race teams get several practice sessions on the track. They tune their cars and try new strategies. Drivers try to find the fastest way around the track. Race teams try to find small adjustments that make the cars handle better. Teams figure out how many laps they can finish on one tank of gas. They also try to find any problems with the car so they can fix them before the race begins.

On Sunday the stands fill with

Car Handling

The way a stock car handles is almost as important as how fast it can go. A driver doesn't want a car that is too "tight" or too "loose." A tight car won't turn easily. The driver has to slow down too much to turn. A loose car turns easily, but the back end doesn't stick to the track well. A driver can easily lose control of a loose car and spin.

fans. Drivers steer their cars onto the track in rows of two. They make several warm-up laps, then watch for a racing official to wave the green flag that starts the race. The drivers stomp down on their accelerators, and the race is on.

Cautions and Pit Stops

Stock car races can be as long as 600 miles and run about three to four hours. Drivers don't spend the whole race speeding around the track.

Cars speed across the
starting line as another
exciting NASCAR race
begins.

GFS MARKETPLACE 400

The pit crew for Carl Edwards's Number 99 car springs into action.

Accidents and bad weather can bring out yellow flags, or cautions. During a caution, a pace car comes onto the track. The drivers line up and follow the pace car at a slow speed.

Pit stops are common during cautions. They also can take place during regular green-flag racing. During a pit stop, the driver pulls the car off the main track onto a pit road. There, every team has a pit stall, like a parking space. When the driver pulls into the pit stall, the pit crew rushes out to work on the car. The pit crew changes the car's tires, adds fuel, and may make small adjustments or repairs. They even give the driver food or water if he wants it. A good pit crew can change all four tires and fill the car with fuel in about 14 seconds. Fast pit stops are a key to winning a race. Drivers can't afford to waste even a second during a stop. A driver who has spent all day passing cars on the track can quickly fall behind with a slow pit stop.

Pit Crews

On race day, the pit crew *(above)* is as important as the driver. Most pit stops start with the jack man. This crew member uses a car jack to raise the car. The tire changer rushes to take off the old tire. A tire carrier carries the new tire to the tire changer and rolls away the old tire. Each pit crew has two tire changers and two tire carriers—one pair for the front tires and another for the rear tires. Once the tires on one side of the car are changed, the jack man rushes to the other side of the car and the process starts over. While the tires are being changed, the car must also be fueled. The gas man fills the car from a large container. The catch can man helps the fueler. This crew member catches the extra fuel that spills out once the car's fuel tank is full. When everything is done, the jack man drops the jack. This is the driver's signal to take off and return to the track.

Tracks

Stock car races take place on many different types of tracks. This is part of what makes the sport so much fun. Oval tracks are the most common in the Nextel Cup. The ovals come in many different types. Talladega Superspeedway is the biggest oval at more than 2.6 miles around. Meanwhile, Bristol Motor Speedway in Tennessee is only half a mile around. Drivers need very different strategies to win at these different tracks.

Track shapes also vary. Martinsville Speedway in Virginia is shaped like a paper clip. Pocono Raceway in Pennsylvania is a giant triangle. Tri-oval tracks, such as Kansas Raceway, look something like a lopsided egg.

Banking is another big difference among tracks. Banking is the angle of the track. The track is paved at a slant to help cars turn at higher speeds.

Racing Flags

NASCAR officials use flags to communicate with drivers. A flagman waves a flag from high above the start/finish line. Here are some of the flags.

Green flag: starts a race and restarts a race after a caution

Yellow flag: signals a caution to drivers

Red flag: stops all of the cars. The track is unsafe to drive on due to a bad accident or bad weather.

Black flag: signals a penalty for a driver. Penalties are usually handed out when a driver does something that could cause a serious accident.

White flag: signals the final lap

Checkered flag: signals the end of the race

Jimmie Johnson spins out in his Number 48 car during a race at Richmond International Raceway in Virginia.

Cars barely have to slow down to handle these banked turns. Flat tracks have little or no banking at all. On flat tracks, drivers have to brake a lot more to slow down to make turns.

The road courses in the Nextel Cup series are a different kind of challenge. Road courses such as Watkins Glen International in New

A nasty wreck has totaled Rusty Wallace's Number 2 car. Damage from crashes is expensive to fix. But thanks to the cars' many safety features, injuries are quite rare.

Driver Matt Kenseth and his team celebrate a Nextel Cup race win at Bristol Motor Speedway in Bristol, Connecticut.

York have many twists and turns. Drivers go up and down hills. Road racing is so different from oval racing that some teams bring in special drivers just for the road races.

The Race Team

A driver can't win alone. A race team includes dozens of people, from owners to car builders to tire carriers. The team starts with the owner, who selects the driver and pit crew and assigns them to a team and a car number. The crew chief picks the pit crew and helps choose the people who will build the cars. Engine builders prepare and tune the team's engines. Chassis builders work on the car bodies.

During a race, the driver talks on the radio to the crew chief and to the spotter. The crew chief works with the driver to make strategy decisions. The spotter is a team member who sits high above the track where he can see all the action. The spotter tells the driver when he has to worry about other cars. He warns the driver if there is a crash ahead. He also helps the crew chief make strategy decisions.

DID YOU KNOW?

Top racing teams build a new engine for every race. After a race is finished, they take apart the car's engine and start over.

Dedicated fans show their support for Rusty Wallace and NASCAR.

The Fans

NASCAR fans are among the most die-hard sports fans in the United States. Hundreds of thousands of people attend the bigger races. Some fans follow the drivers from track to track, week to week. They wear shirts and hats with their favorite driver's number. They put decals on their car bumpers and windows. They cheer hard for their driver and boo harder for their driver's biggest rivals.

The Daytona 500, the first race of each year, is the biggest event for NASCAR fans. Many fans show up two weeks before the race. Some spend thousands of dollars to camp out in the track's infield as they wait for the big day. Fans fill the stands to watch all of the prerace events, even the practice sessions. By the time the green flag drops to start the race, almost 200,000 people are standing and cheering. Millions more fans watch on television. Tickets cost $100 or more, but some people at the race are so ex-

Get Behind the Wheel

Few people will ever have a chance to race a real stock car. But people of all ages can enjoy the thrill of racing competition through video games and racing simulators. NASCAR fans can choose from many different NASCAR video games for all of the most popular gaming systems, like the Sony PlayStation series and the X-Box series. But for an even more realistic experience, fans can get behind the wheel of a racing simulator. These machines are built to look exactly like a NASCAR car, inside and out. The simulator creates the same sound, motion, and rush that NASCAR drivers experience on race day.

cited that they never even bother to sit down in their seats.

For these die-hard fans, NASCAR is about more than just racing. It's part of a thrilling experience, a part of a culture and tradition that is uniquely American. NASCAR isn't just a sport. It's a way of life.

The crowd roars as their favorite drivers fight for position at Lowe's Motor Speedway in North Carolina.

NASCAR Tracks

NASCAR cars and trucks compete on more than 30 tracks across the United States. Most ovals are different lengths and shapes. Here is a sampling of NASCAR tracks, including the circuit's two road courses, and their locations.

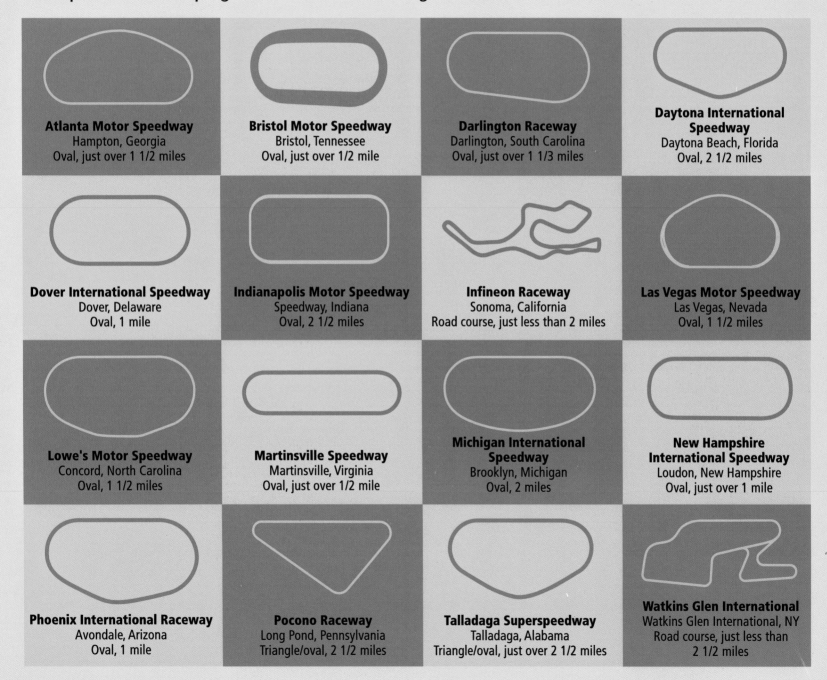

Atlanta Motor Speedway
Hampton, Georgia
Oval, just over 1 1/2 miles

Bristol Motor Speedway
Bristol, Tennessee
Oval, just over 1/2 mile

Darlington Raceway
Darlington, South Carolina
Oval, just over 1 1/3 miles

Daytona International Speedway
Daytona Beach, Florida
Oval, 2 1/2 miles

Dover International Speedway
Dover, Delaware
Oval, 1 mile

Indianapolis Motor Speedway
Speedway, Indiana
Oval, 2 1/2 miles

Infineon Raceway
Sonoma, California
Road course, just less than 2 miles

Las Vegas Motor Speedway
Las Vegas, Nevada
Oval, 1 1/2 miles

Lowe's Motor Speedway
Concord, North Carolina
Oval, 1 1/2 miles

Martinsville Speedway
Martinsville, Virginia
Oval, just over 1/2 mile

Michigan International Speedway
Brooklyn, Michigan
Oval, 2 miles

New Hampshire International Speedway
Loudon, New Hampshire
Oval, just over 1 mile

Phoenix International Raceway
Avondale, Arizona
Oval, 1 mile

Pocono Raceway
Long Pond, Pennsylvania
Triangle/oval, 2 1/2 miles

Talladaga Superspeedway
Talladaga, Alabama
Triangle/oval, just over 2 1/2 miles

Watkins Glen International
Watkins Glen International, NY
Road course, just less than 2 1/2 miles

NASCAR Tracks in the United States

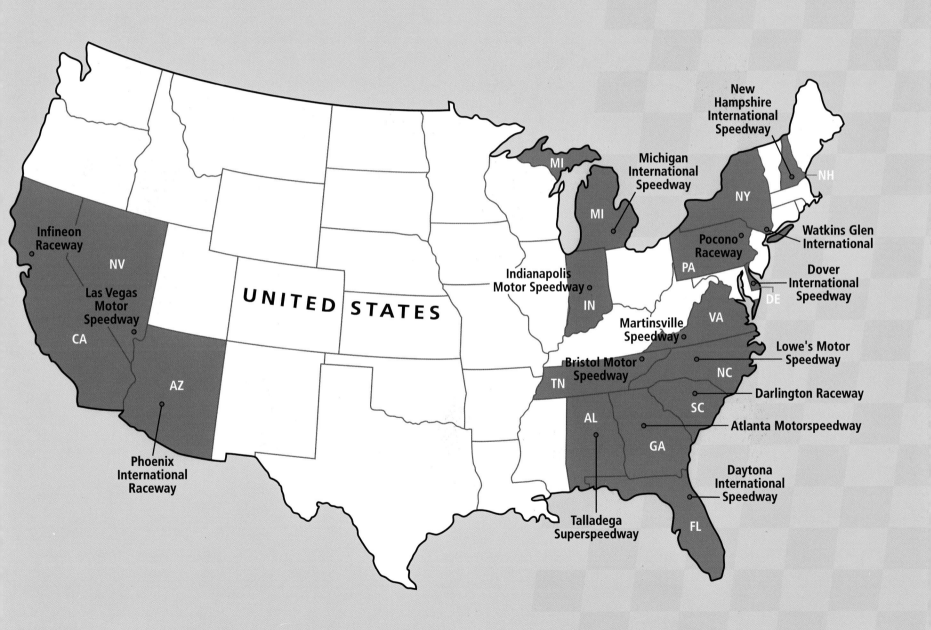

New Hampshire International Speedway

Michigan International Speedway

Watkins Glen International

Pocono Raceway

Dover International Speedway

Indianapolis Motor Speedway

Lowe's Motor Speedway

Martinsville Speedway

Darlington Raceway

Bristol Motor Speedway

Atlanta Motorspeedway

Infineon Raceway

Las Vegas Motor Speedway

Daytona International Speedway

Phoenix International Raceway

Talladega Superspeedway

UNITED STATES

NV · NY · MI · MI · NH · PA · IN · DE · VA · NC · SC · GA · AL · FL · TN · CA · AZ

Bobby Allison (born 1937)

Bobby Allison won a championship in 1983, but he's best known for finishing in second place. Allison was NASCAR's runner-up five times in his career. He was named NASCAR's most popular driver six times. Allison retired after a 1988 accident.

Seasons: 1961,1965–1988

Wins: 85

Top-5s: 336

Poles: 57

Championships: 1

Dale Earnhardt (1951–2001)

The Intimidator was one of the most popular and talented drivers in NASCAR history. Earnhardt was the dominant driver throughout the 1980s and early 1990s, when he won seven championships before his death at the 2001 Daytona 500. Earnhardt's sons, Dale Jr. and Kerry, are both NASCAR drivers.

Seasons: 1975–2001

Wins: 76

Top-5s: 281

Poles: 22

Championships: 7

Bobby Allison's Number 15 car

Dale Earnhardt's Number 3 car

Dale Earnhardt Jr. (born 1974)

The son of a NASCAR legend quickly made a name for himself by winning the Busch Series title in each of his first two seasons. Since joining the Winston Cup/Nextel Cup series in 1999, Junior has dominated at Daytona and Talladega, at one point winning four straight Talladega races.

Seasons: 1999–

Wins: 16

Top-5s: 59

Poles: 6

Championships: 0

Jeff Gordon (born 1971)

Jeff Gordon is probably the best driver in modern NASCAR. He started his career in 1992 and quickly rose to the top. In 1998—his greatest season—Gordon won 13 races, including four in a row at one point. In 2004 he barely missed winning his fifth championship.

Seasons: 1992–

Wins: 73

Top-5s: 198

Poles: 54

Championships: 4

Dale Earnhardt Jr.'s Number 8 car

Jeff Gordon's Number 24 car

Jimmie Johnson (born 1975)

One of NASCAR's hottest drivers, Johnson finished second in points in both 2003 and 2004. After making his name racing off-road cars, Johnson made his debut on the Busch Series circuit for the 1999 season. Three successful seasons in the Busch circuit earned him a ride in NASCAR's top circuit. He finished second in rookie-of-the-year voting in 2002 and has continued to tear up the track since.

Seasons: 2001–
Wins: 18
Top-5s: 54
Poles: 12
Championships: 0

David Pearson (born 1934)

David Pearson, called the Silver Fox by fans and fellow drivers, is second only to Richard Petty on NASCAR's all-time win list with 105. Pearson's best season may have been 1973, when he won 11 of the 18 races he entered.

Seasons: 1960–1986
Wins: 105
Top-5s: 301
Poles: 113
Championships: 3

Jimmie Johnson's Number 48 car

David Pearson's Number 21 car

Richard Petty (born 1937)

Many NASCAR fans call Richard Petty the king of stock car racing. His 35-year career began in 1958. In 1967 he had the greatest season in NASCAR history, winning 27 of 48 races, including 10 in a row.

Seasons: 1958–1992

Wins: 200

Top-5s: 555

Poles: 126

Championships: 7

Fireball Roberts (1929–1964)

Most experts call Edward Glenn "Fireball" Roberts the best driver to never win a championship. Roberts's 15-year career was cut short in 1964 when an accident trapped him in a burning car. He later died because of his injuries.

Seasons: 1950–1964

Wins: 32

Top-5s: 93

Poles: 35

Championships: 0

Richard Petty's Number 43 car

Fireball Roberts's Number 22 car

Tony Stewart (born 1971)

Tony Stewart was a racing champion long before he ever sat inside a stock car. Stewart won two Indy Racing League (IRL) titles in the mid-1990s before switching to stock cars full-time. He won his first NASCAR title in 2002 and is considered one of the best NASCAR drivers on short tracks and road courses.

Seasons: 1999–

Wins: 24

Top-5s: 93

Poles: 12

Championships: 2

Rusty Wallace (born 1956)

Rusty Wallace's career began with a bang. In 1980 he finished second in the first Winston Cup race he ever drove in. In 1984, his first full year in Winston Cup, he was named Rookie of the Year. Five years later, he won his only championship.

Seasons: 1980–

Wins: 55

Top-5s: 202

Poles: 36

Championships: 1

Tony Stewart's Number 20 car

Rusty Wallace's Number 2 car

Darrell Waltrip (born 1947)

During the 1980s, the only driver to consistently challenge Dale Earnhardt was Darrell Waltrip. One of the sport's most popular drivers, Waltrip is now an announcer for Fox network's Nextel Cup TV broadcasts. His younger brother, Michael, is a popular driver.

Seasons: 1972–2000
Wins: 84
Top-5s: 276
Poles: 59
Championships: 3

Cale Yarborough (born 1939)

Cale Yarborough was the dominant driver of the mid-1970s. He is the only driver to ever win three straight championships (1976–1978). In 1984 Yarborough became the first driver to qualify for the Daytona 500 at more than 200 miles per hour.

Seasons: 1957, 1959–1988
Wins: 83
Top-5s: 255
Poles: 70
Championships: 3

Darrell Waltrip's Number 95 car

Cale Yarborough's Number 11 car

Glossary

aerodynamic: the physical quality of a vehicle that allows air to flow easily over its surface

banking: the inward slope of a track's turns

bootleggers: people who illegally made or sold alcohol during Prohibition, a time in the early 1900s when the United States outlawed alcohol.

caution: a period during a race when the track is not safe to drive at full speed. Accidents and bad weather can cause cautions.

chassis: the main body, or frame, of a stock car

cylinder: a hollow tube in which gas and air are compressed by a piston as part of the process that produces an engine's power

horsepower: a measure of an engine's power

pace car: the car that comes onto the track during a caution period to lead the racecars at a slow, safe speed

pole: the first starting spot for a race

roll cage: a system of strong bars that surrounds the driver in a stock car. The roll cage prevents the car from collapsing and crushing the driver.

slicks: smooth, soft tires for racing

superspeedway: a very large oval track with banked turns

traction: the grip of a vehicle's tires to the driving surface

Selected Bibliography

Center, Bill. *NASCAR: The Thunder of America*. New York: HarperHorizon, 1998.

Golenbock, Peter, ed. *Nascar Encyclopedia*. Saint Paul: Motorbooks International, 2003.

Hembree, Michael. *NASCAR: The Definitive History of America's Sport*. New York: HarperEntertainment, 2000.

Martin, Mark, and Beth Tuschak. *NASCAR for Dummies*. Hoboken, NJ: Wiley, 2005.

Menzer, Joe. *The Wildest Ride: A History of NASCAR (or, How a Bunch of Good Ol' Boys Built a Billion-Dollar Industry out of Wrecking Cars)*. New York: Simon & Schuster, 2001.

Johnstone, Michael. *NASCAR*. Minneapolis: LernerSports, 2002.

Piehl, Janet. *Formula One Race Cars*. Minneapolis: Lerner Publication Company, 2007.

Raby, Philip. *Racing Cars*. Minneapolis: LernerSports, 1999.

Savage, Jeff. *Dale Earnhardt Jr.* Minneapolis: Lerner Publications Company, 2006.

Savage, Jeff. *Jeff Gordon*. Minneapolis: Lerner Publications Company, 2003.

Further Reading

Braun, Eric. *Hot Rods*. Minneapolis: Lerner Publications Company, 2007.

Buckley, James. *NASCAR*. New York: DK Publishing, 2005.

Doeden, Matt. *Dale Earnhardt Jr.* Minneapolis: Lerner Publications Company, 2005.

Websites

Daytona International Speedway
http://www.daytona500.com

The site of NASCAR's most famous track includes racing news, facts about the Daytona 500 race, and detailed diagrams of the track.

NASCAR
http://www.nascar.com

NASCAR's official website includes news, racing schedules, results, interviews, driver statistics, and more.

Index

About the Author

Matt Doeden is a freelance author and editor and an avid NASCAR fan. He has written more than 40 books, including several on stock car racing and its drivers.

About the Consultant

William Burt is a freelance author based in Anniston, Alabama. He has written several books about NASCAR stock cars and NASCAR drivers.

Photo Acknowledgments

The images in this book are used with the permission of: © Artemis Images, pp. 4–5, 16 (top), 17 (bottom), 19, 20 (background), 21, 24, 35 (top and bottom), 36 (bottom), 37 (top and bottom), 39 (top and bottom), 41 (top), 42 (top and bottom), 43 (top and bottom), 45 (bottom); Library of Congress, p. 6 (foreground and background); Detroit Public Library, Automotive History Collection, p. 7; © Darrell Ingham/Getty Images, p. 9; Laura Westlund, pp. 11, 32, 33; © Bettmann/CORBIS, pp. 14, 34 (top), 38 (bottom), 40 (top and bottom), 41 (bottom), 44 (top and bottom); © Rob Tringali/SportsChrome, pp.15 (top), 25; © Jerry Howell/ZUMA Press, p. 15 (bottom); © Frank Polich/Icon SMI, p.16 (bottom); © Reuters/CORBIS, pp. 17 (top), 18, 34 (bottom); © Irwin Thompson/*Dallas Morning News*/CORBIS, p. 22; © Worth Canoy/Icon SMI, pp. 23, 29; © Jamie Squire/Getty Images, p. 27; © Joe Skipper/Reuters/CORBIS, p. 28; © David Taylor/Getty Images, p. 30; © George Tiedemann/NewSport/CORBIS, p. 31; © Joe Robbins-US PRESS-WIRE/ZUMA Press, pp.36 (top), 38 (top); © AP/Wide World Photos, p. 45 (top). Front Cover: © George Tiedemann/NewSport/CORBIS.